ABC Activity Book

for ages 3-5

This CGP book is full of bright and colourful activities for pre-school and Reception children.

It's a brilliant way to introduce the letters of the alphabet — and it's stacks of fun too!

 # Hints for Helpers

Here are a few useful things to know when using this book:

- This book contains practice to help children learn to recognise the letters of the alphabet. You can help your child by reading the instructions out loud and encouraging them to sound out letters.

- It is often helpful to use letter sounds with your child, rather than letter names. For example, if you see the letter 'b', you should say 'buh', not 'bee'.

- The activities in this book encourage children to say letter sounds. Some sounds are trickier than others, so don't worry if your child doesn't know every sound. You can help them by sounding out any letters they don't know.

- Each page includes tracing practice to help children become more familiar with letters. Encourage your child to trace with their finger first, then ask them to try with a pencil. Your child can use their right or left hand — whichever they find easier.

- For each letter, there is a dot showing where to start and arrows to follow to complete the letter.

- Bear in mind that every nursery or school has its own handwriting style. Some schools may form letters differently to how they're written here — for example, k instead of k.

- This book is designed to be worked through in order. However, the 'Cloud clues' activity in the centre uses letters from the whole book. You may want to complete this activity last.

Contents

The letter a	2	The letter m	16
The letter b	3	The letter n	17
The letter c	4	The letter o	18
The letter d	5	The letter p	19
The letter e	6	The letter q	20
The letter f	7	The letter r	21
The letter g	8	The letter s	22
The letter h	9	The letter t	23
The letter i	10	The letters u and v	24
The letter j	11	The letter w	25
The letter k	12	The letters x, y and z	26
The letter l	13	Letter practice	27
Cloud clues	14	Marvellous maze	30

Published by CGP

Editors: Emma Cleasby, Becca Lakin, Georgina Paxman

With thanks to Andy Cashmore and Gareth Mitchell for the proofreading.

With thanks to Emily Smith for the copyright research.

ISBN: 978 1 78908 892 2

Printed by Elanders Ltd, Newcastle upon Tyne.
Graphics used on the cover and throughout the book © Educlips
Cover design concept by emc design ltd.

Text, design, layout and original illustrations © Coordination Group Publications Ltd. (CGP) 2022
All rights reserved.

Photocopying this book is not permitted, even if you have a CLA licence.
Extra copies are available from CGP with next day delivery • 0800 1712 712 • www.cgpbooks.co.uk

The letter a

First Look at This

Try tracing the letters. Start at the red dots and follow the arrows. What sound does this letter make?

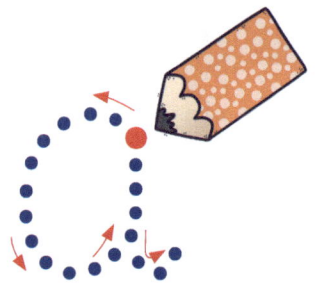
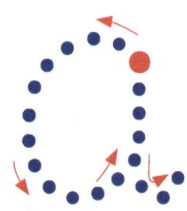

Now Try This

Colour in the apples that have the letter **a** on them.

Amazing — you've learnt the letter a. Colour the smiley face.

The letter b

First Look at This

Practise tracing the letters. Trace with your finger first. Then try with a pencil. Do you know what sound this letter makes?

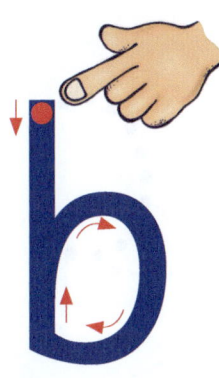 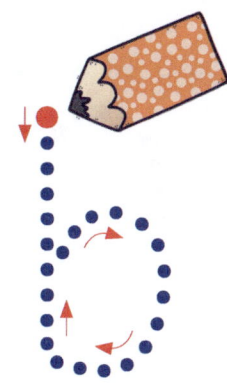 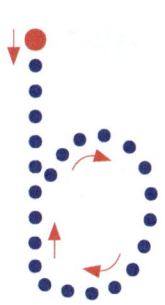

Now Try This

What things can you see on the shelves? Say them out loud. Circle all of the things that start with the letter **b**.

Wow! That was beautifully done. Colour the smiley face.

The letter c

First Look at This

Have a go at tracing the letters.
Do you know what sound this letter makes?

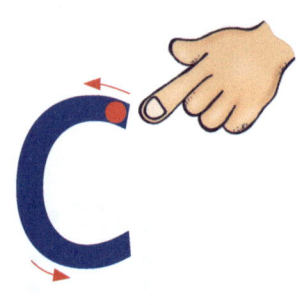
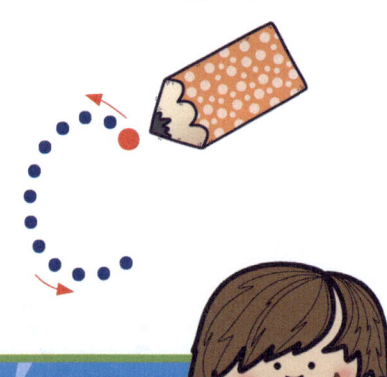
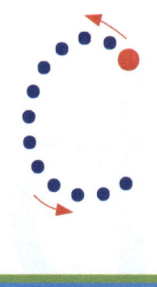

Now Try This

Say the names of these things that Max sees on his way to school.
Draw lines to match the pictures that start with **c** to the letter **c**.

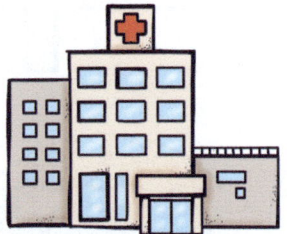

Congratulations! You know the letter c. Colour the smiley face.

The letter d

First Look at This

Practise tracing the letters.
Can you say the sound this letter makes?

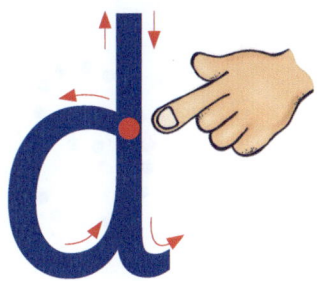 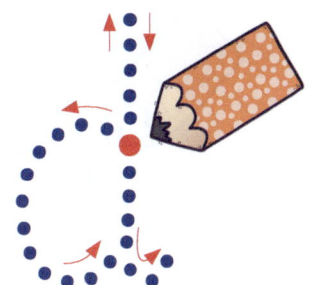 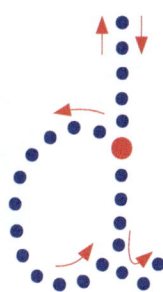

Now Try This

Colour in the boxes that have the letter **d** in them.

Hooray — this page is done and dusted. Colour the smiley face.

The letter e

First Look at This

Practise tracing the letters.
Do you know what sound this letter makes?

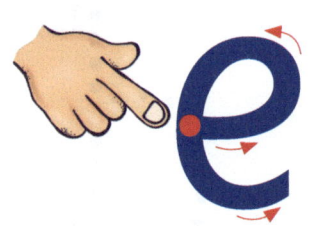 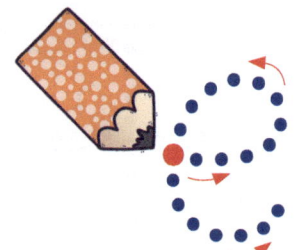 

Now Try This

Trace the path that starts with the letter **e**.
Which egg does the path lead to? Circle the egg.

Excellent! You've learnt the letter e. Colour the smiley face.

The letter f

First Look at This

Try tracing the letters. Can you say the sound this letter makes?

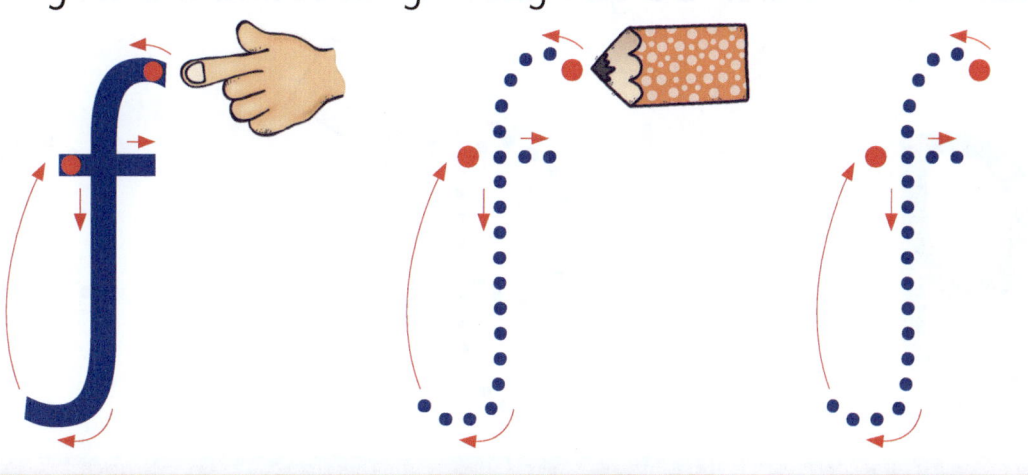

Now Try This

Can you say the names of the animals?
Circle all of the animals that start with the letter **f**.

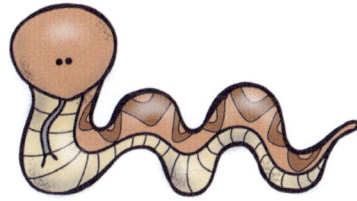

You flew through this page — fantastic! Colour the smiley face.

The letter g

First Look at This

Try tracing the letters. Do you know what sound this letter makes?

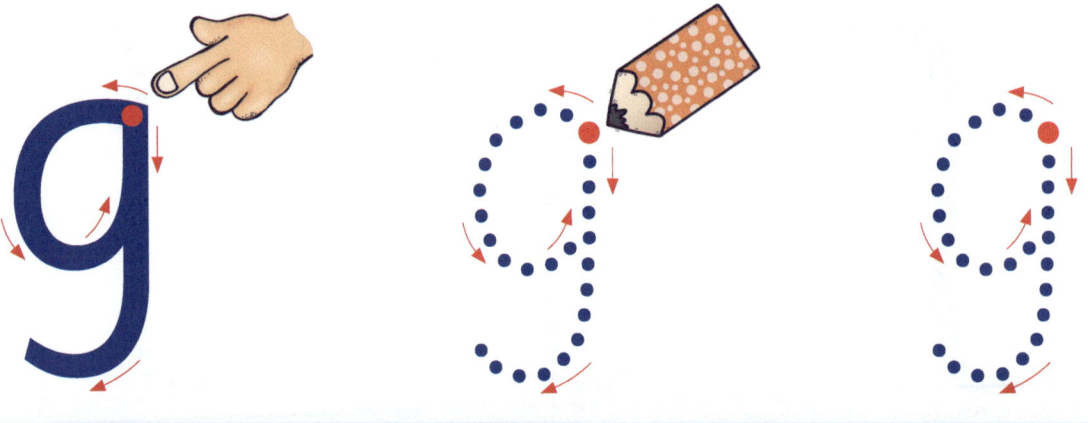

Now Try This

Colour the boxes that have the letter **g** in them.

Great work! You know the letter g. Colour the smiley face.

The letter h

First Look at This

Trace the letters. Can you say the sound this letter makes?

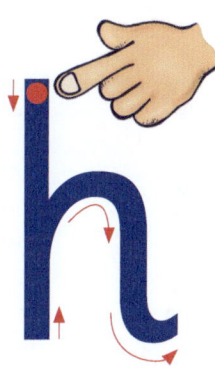 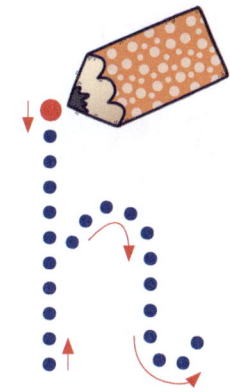 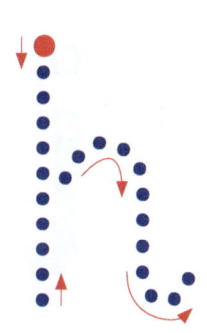

Now Try This

What things can you see in the picture? Say them aloud. Colour the things that start with the letter **h**.

Hooray! You've learnt the letter h. Colour the smiley face.

The letter i

First Look at This

Try tracing the letters. Don't forget to give the **i** a dot.
Can you say the sound this letter makes?

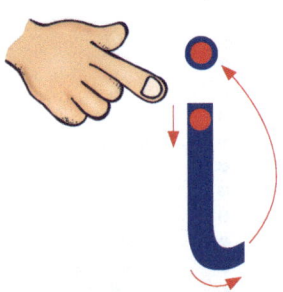 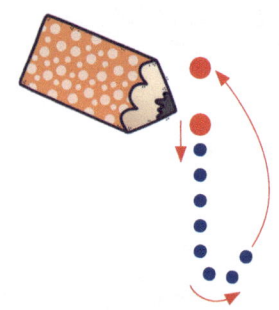 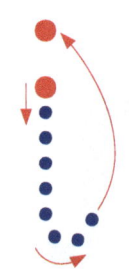

Now Try This

Colour the ice creams that have the letter **i** on them.

Draw a line to match the two pictures with the letter **i** on them.

 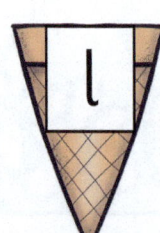 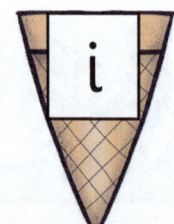 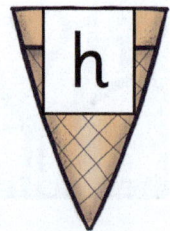

Good job! You've learnt the letter i. Colour the smiley face.

The letter j

First Look at This

Practise tracing the letters. Don't forget the dots.
Do you know what sound this letter makes?

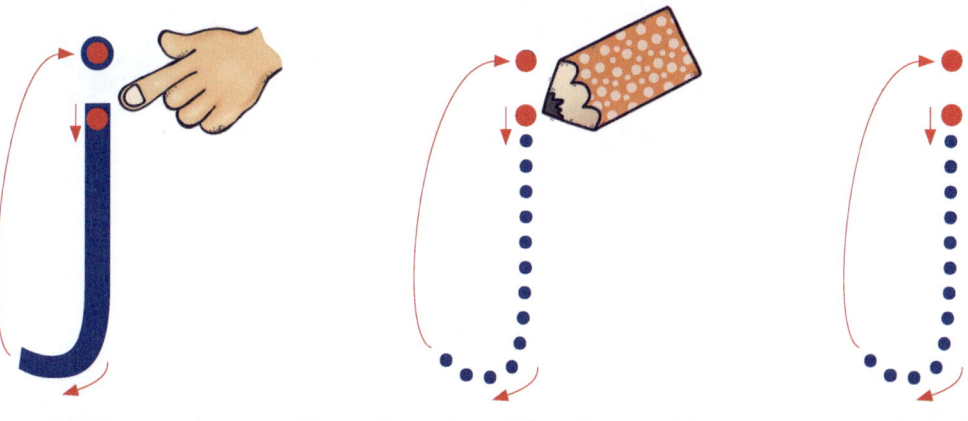

Now Try This

Colour the boxes that have the letter **j** in them.

j   a   b   j

e   j   p

What a treat — you know the letter j. Colour the smiley face.

The letter k

First Look at This

Try tracing the letters. Can you say the sound this letter makes?

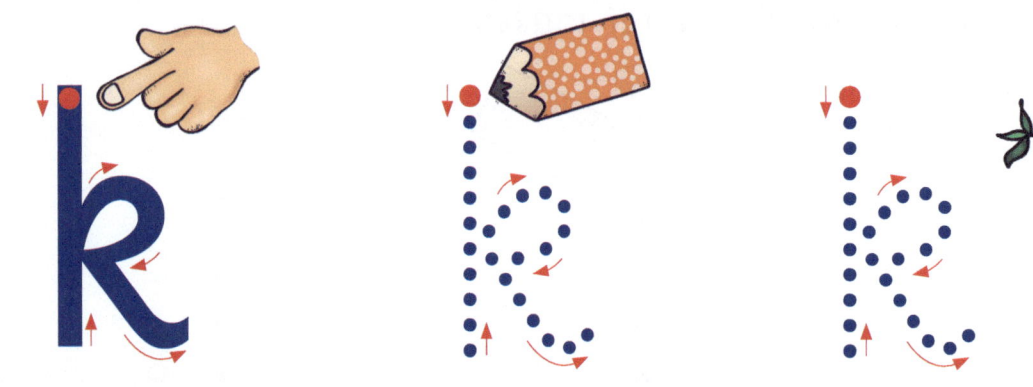

Now Try This

Colour the mouth that has the letter **k** in it.

Circle all the paw prints that have the letter **k** on them.

Well done! You know the letter k. Colour the smiley face.

The letter l

First Look at This

Trace the letters. Do you know the sound this letter makes?

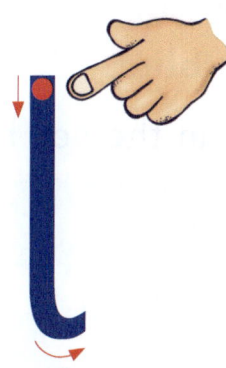
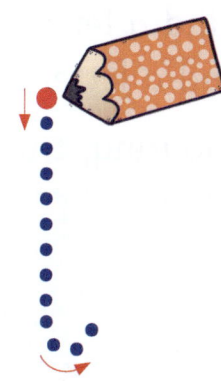

Now Try This

Can you say the words for the pictures? Find all the things that start with **l**. Draw lines to match them to the letter **l**.

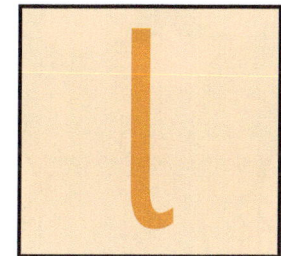

Amazing — you've learnt the letter l. Colour the smiley face.

Cloud clues

What letters can you see in the sky in the picture?
When you find a letter **g**, colour it in **green**.
When you find a letter **r**, colour it in **red**.
When you find a letter **b**, colour it in **blue**.

When you've finished colouring, try the question in the box below.

There is one letter left that has not been coloured in.
Do you know what it is? Tick the box next to the letter.

The letter m

First Look at This

Try tracing the letters. Do you know what sound this letter makes?

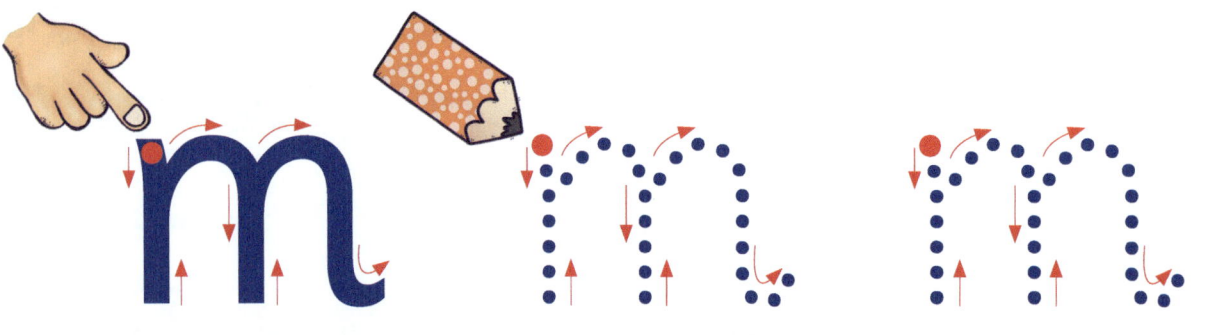

Now Try This

Circle the medals that have the letter **m** on them.

Colour in the person who is wearing the letter **m**.

Marvellous! You're so great at this. Colour the smiley face.

The letter n

First Look at This

Practise tracing the letters.
Can you say the sound this letter makes?

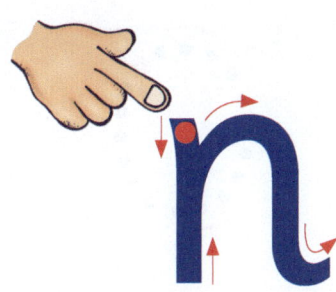
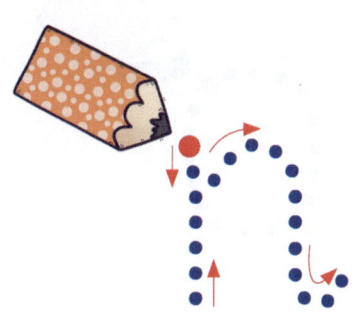
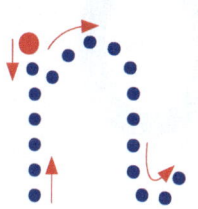

Now Try This

What things can you see in the picture? Say their names out loud.
How many things can you spot that start with the letter **n**?

Nice job! You know the letter n now. Colour the smiley face.

The letter o

First Look at This

Try tracing the letters. Do you know what sound this letter makes?

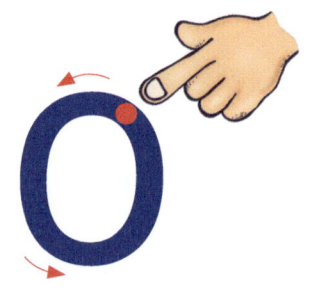 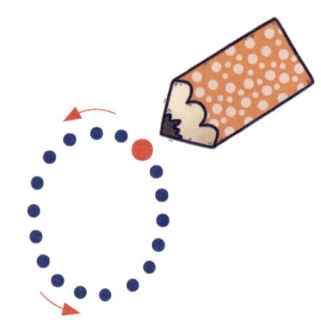 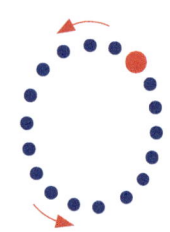

Now Try This

Colour the train carriages that have the letter **o** on them.

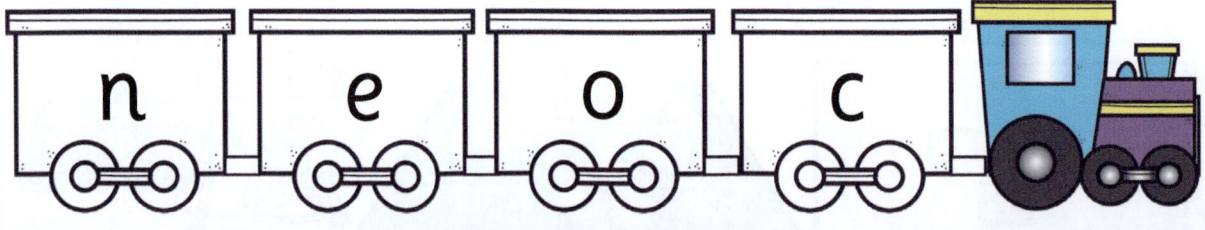

Outstanding! Another page finished. Colour the smiley face.

The letter p

First Look at This

Try tracing the letters. Can you say the sound this letter makes?

 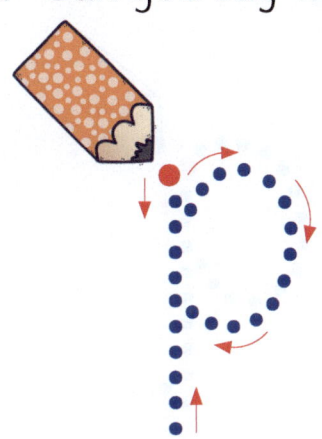 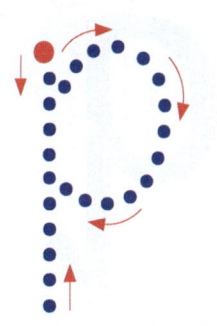

Now Try This

Can you say the words for the pictures? Find all the things that start with **p**. Draw lines to match them to the letter **p**.

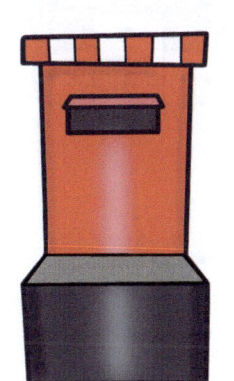  

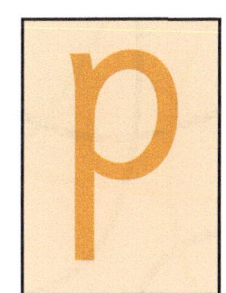

 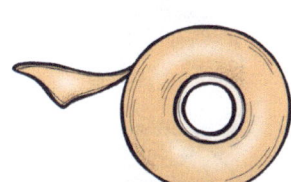 

Perfect! You know the letter p now. Colour the smiley face.

The letter q

First Look at This

Try tracing the letters. Can you say the sound this letter makes?

 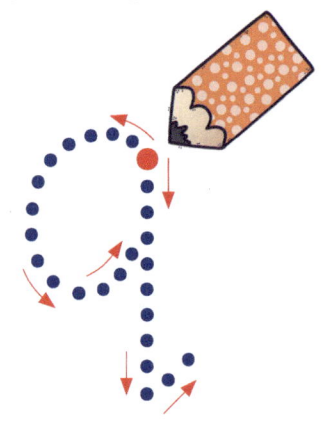 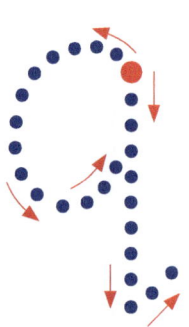

Now Try This

Trace the path that starts with the letter **q**.
Which queen does the path lead to? Circle the queen.

Well done! You are queen of the letter q. Colour the smiley face.

The letter r

First Look at This

Trace the letters. Do you know what sound this letter makes?

Now Try This

What things can you see in the picture? Say them aloud. Colour the things that start with the letter **r**.

Remarkable! You're really good at this. Colour the smiley face.

The letter s

First Look at This

Try tracing the letters. Can you say the sound this letter makes?

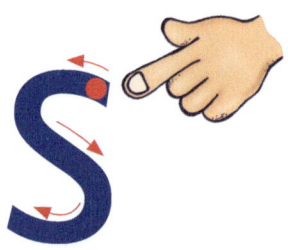 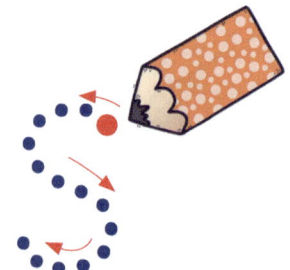 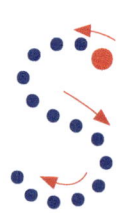

Now Try This

What can you see in the pictures?
Tick the box under the pictures that start with the letter **s**.

Superb! Now you know the letter s. Colour the smiley face.

The letter t

First Look at This

Practise tracing the letters. What sound does this letter make?

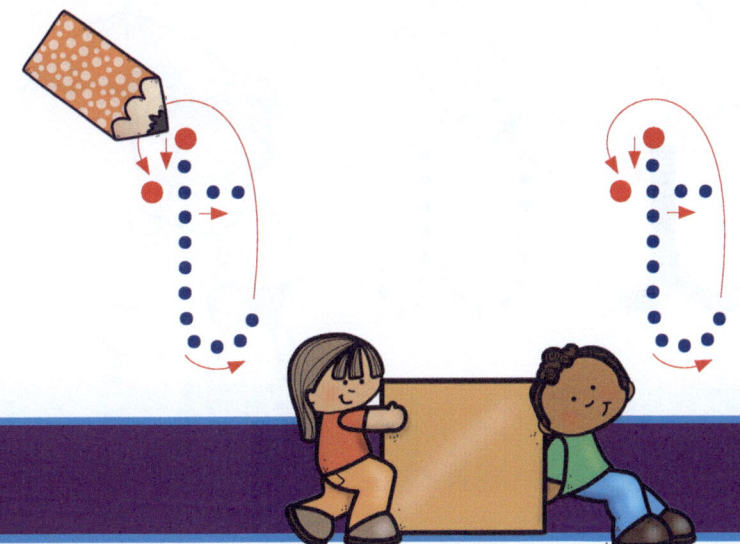

Now Try This

Can you say the words for the pictures?
Colour in all of the things that start with the letter **t**.

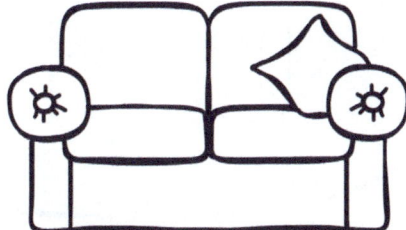

Terrific work! You've learnt the letter t. Colour the smiley face.

The letters u and v

First Look at This

Trace the letters. Do you know what sound each letter makes?

Now Try This

Colour the boxes with the letter **u** in **red**.
Colour the boxes with the letter **v** in **blue**.

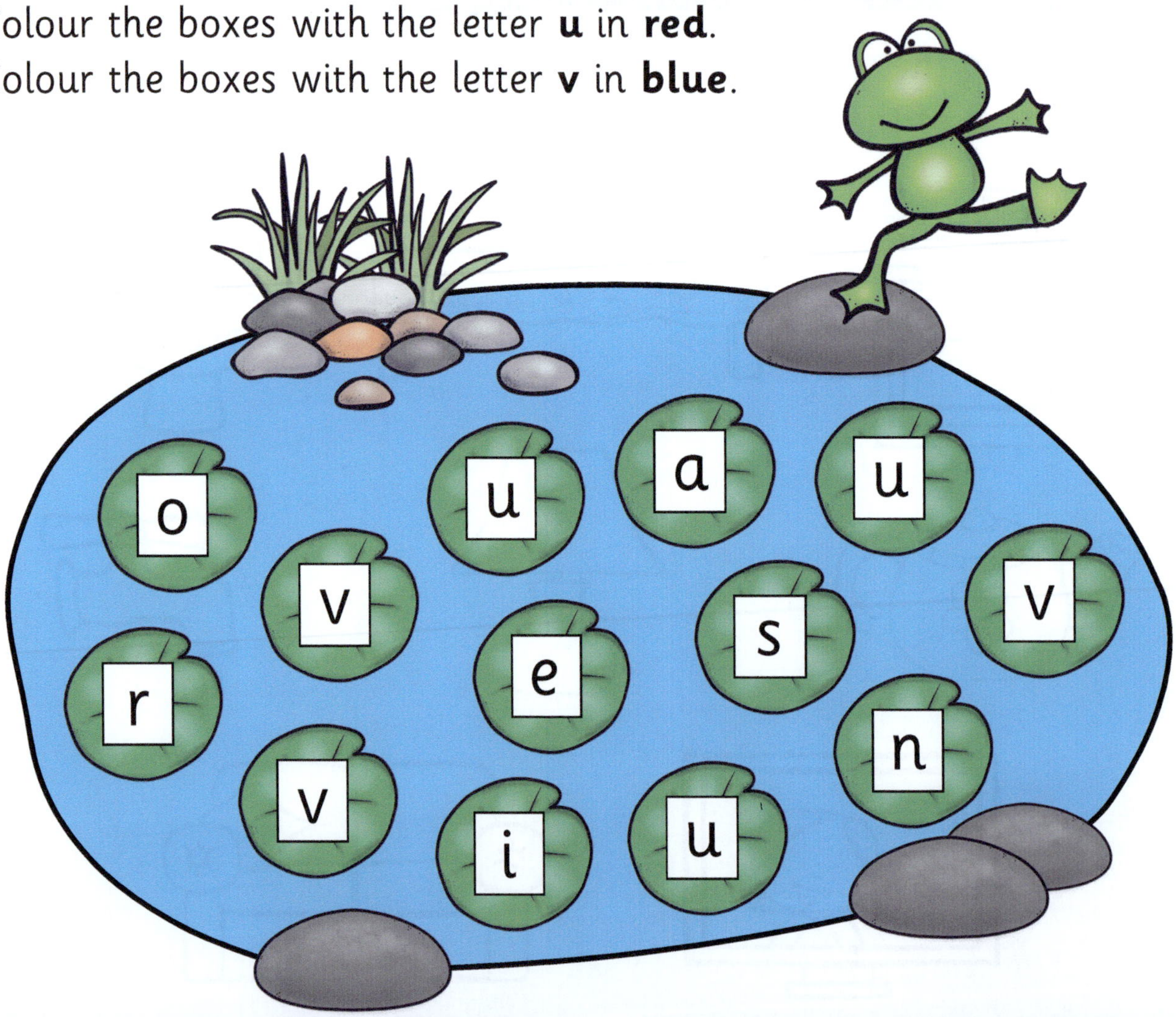

Fantastic – you leapt through this page. Colour the smiley face.

The letter w

First Look at This

Try tracing the letters. Do you know what sound this letter makes?

 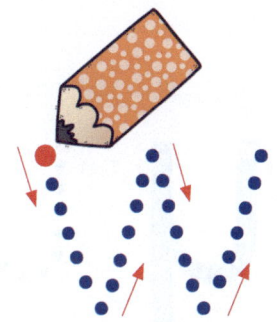 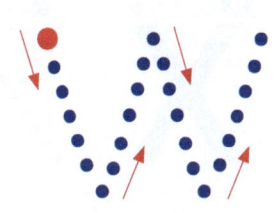

Now Try This

Can you say the words for the pictures? Find all the things that start with **w**. Draw lines to match them to the letter **w**.

Well done! You've learnt the letter w. Colour the smiley face.

# The letters x, y and z

First Look at This

Try tracing the letters. Do you know what sound each letter makes?

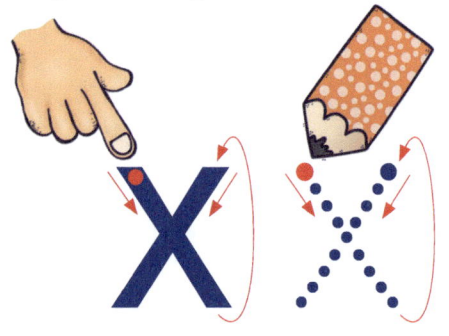 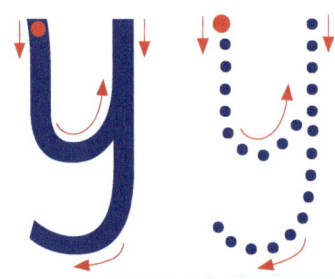 

Now Try This

Trace the path that starts at **x**. Colour the drum it leads to in **red**.
Trace the path that starts at **y**. Colour the drum it leads to in **blue**.
Trace the path that starts at **z**. Colour the drum it leads to in **green**.

Yippee! You've done an amazing job. Colour the smiley face.

Letter practice

First Look at This

Look at the letters in the rings.
What sound does each letter make?

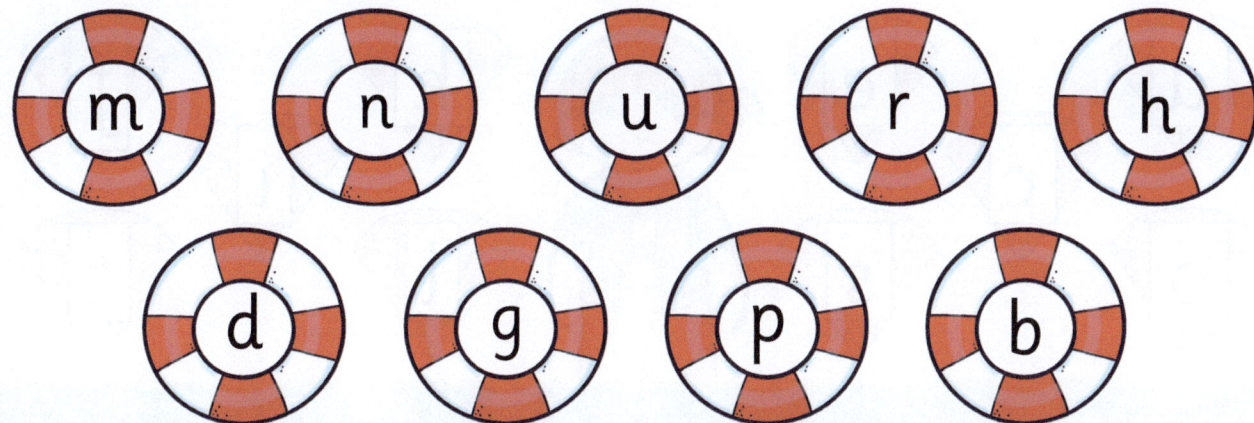

Now Try This

Can you find **four** pairs of matching letters in the picture?
Draw lines to join each pair of letters together.

Hooray! Give yourself a pat on the back. Colour the smiley face.

Letter practice

First Look at This

Look at the letters in the jewels.
What sound does each letter make?

Now Try This

Circle the rings that contain the letter **l**.

Can you match each thing to the letter it starts with?

Wow! You sailed through this page. Colour the smiley face.

Letter practice

First Look at This

You can put letters together to make words.
Say the sound each letter makes, then trace the letters.

Now Try This

Colour in the cats holding the letters **c**, **a** and **t**.

Circle the dogs holding the letters **d**, **o** and **g**.

Excellent work! You are pawesome. Colour the smiley face.

Marvellous maze

Oh no — Aisha is stuck in the maze! Can you help her get out? Colour in the squares with the letters **m**, **a**, **z** and **e** on them to show the way out.